# MAZE QUEST

## HISTORY

CARLTON
KiDS

THIS IS A CARLTON BOOK

Text, design and illustration © Carlton Books Limited 2018

Published in 2018 by Carlton Books Limited,
An imprint of the Carlton Publishing Group,
20 Mortimer Street, London W1T 3JW

Author: Anna Brett                    Illustrator: Tom Woolley
Executive Editor: Selina Wood         Design Manager: Emily Clarke
Production: Nicola Davey              Designers: Claire Clewley, Rachel Lawston

A catalogue record for this book is available from the British Library.

ISBN: 978-1-78312-413-8
Printed and bound in China

# MAZE QUEST
## HISTORY

# How to use this book

Have you ever wished you could time travel and visit the age of the dinosaurs, the Ancient Egyptians or be at the first landing on the Moon? Then you'll be keen to join George and Milly on an incredible maze quest through time! This is how you do it...

# The big picture...

History is all about people and events from the past. Each maze on your quest takes you to a destination in history - and some even in the future! On the left-hand pages, read fascinating facts and stats about each place you visit. Learn about famous historical events, people and objects, and discover what the future may hold.

# Things to spot

Keep an eye out for the things to spot on each maze. To find the correct route through each maze, you'll need to pass closely each of the things listed on the left-hand pages.

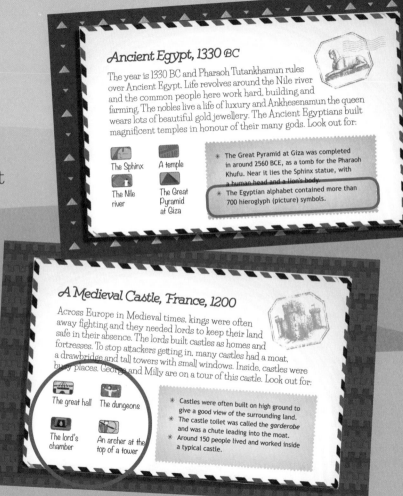

## Ancient Egypt, 1330 BC

The year is 1330 BC and Pharaoh Tutankhamun rules over Ancient Egypt. Life revolves around the Nile river and the common people here work hard, building and farming. The nobles live a life of luxury and Ankhesenamun the queen wears lots of beautiful gold jewellery. The Ancient Egyptians built magnificent temples in honour of their many gods. Look out for:

The Sphinx    A temple

The Nile river    The Great Pyramid at Giza

* The Great Pyramid at Giza was completed in around 2560 BCE, as a tomb for the Pharaoh Khufu. Near it lies the Sphinx statue, with a human head and a lion's body.
* The Egyptian alphabet contained more than 700 hieroglyph (picture) symbols.

## A Medieval Castle, France, 1200

Across Europe in Medieval times, kings were often away fighting and they needed lords to keep their land safe in their absence. The lords built castles as homes and fortresses. To stop attackers getting in, many castles had a moat, a drawbridge and tall towers with small windows. Inside, castles were busy places. George and Milly are on a tour of this castle. Look out for:

The great hall    The dungeons

The lord's chamber    An archer at the top of a tower

* Castles were often built on high ground to give a good view of the surrounding land.
* The castle toilet was called the *garderobe* and was a chute leading into the moat.
* Around 150 people lived and worked inside a typical castle.

George and Milly come across many fascinating objects and symbols from bygone eras as they whizz through time. To get through each maze, look for the object or symbol that was at the end of the last maze. That's your start point! Now make your way to the next object or symbol to find your way out of the maze.

Look for the objects!

Top
tip

Always
follow the main
path and try to
find the shortest
route!

It's time to get started, so turn the page to begin your maze quest. Meet your companions George and Milly at the local Natural History Museum and the rest is up to you! Good luck, have fun and see you at the final destination!

This way...

# A trip to the Natural History Museum

George and Milly are at the Natural History Museum visiting the dinosaurs. Milly is staring at all the bones; George doesn't want her to chew them! While admiring a huge Diplodocus skeleton, George suddenly trips over his shoelace and grabs the tip of the dinosaur's tail to break his fall. In a split second George and Milly are transported back in time! Can you pass the following on the maze to help them on their way?

Neck bones

The small head

The huge claws

The thin, whip-like tail

* George is a Geography teacher who enjoys exploring and who loves cheese sandwiches.
* Milly is George's faithful companion who adores bones and chasing cats!

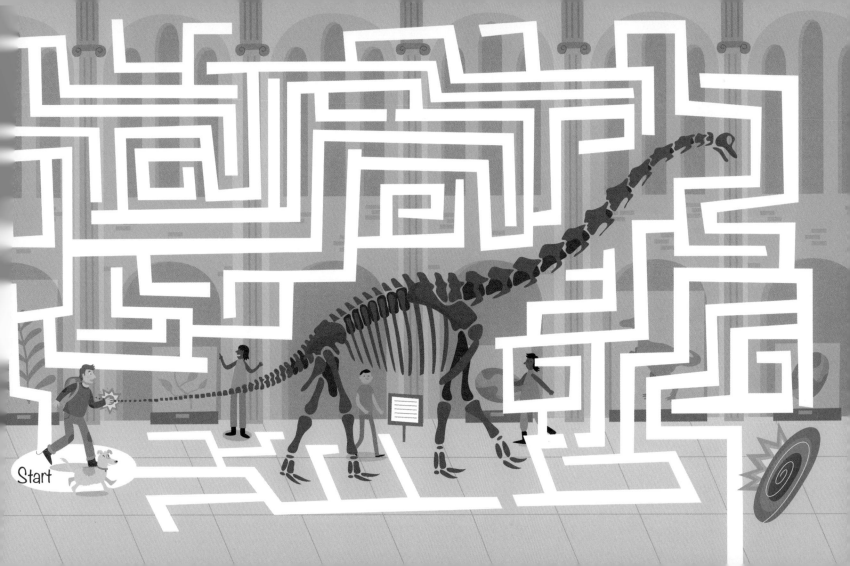

Start

# The Dinosaurs, 150 million years ago

George and Milly have been transported back to the Jurassic age, around 150 million years ago. The land is green and lush and huge dinosaurs roam the planet. George knows they may end up as something's dinner, so they decide to look for a route home. They pass the following:

A fallen tree

A Stegosaurus

A ferocious Allosaurus

A Liopleurodon in the lake

* Plant-eater Stegosaurus had two rows of bony plates along its back up to 60 cm high.
* Meat-eating Allosaurus hunted Stegosaurus and Diplodocus for food.
* The first birds appeared in the Jurassic period in the form of Archaeopteryx.

# An Ice Age, 2.5 million years ago

Brrr! Our friends have reached an Ice Age and it's freezing cold. There's not much life here and they need to escape before they become frozen in time! The northern and southern caps of the Earth are covered in ice that never melts. George and Milly come close to these prehistoric animals on their travels -can you?

 An arctic shrew

 A sabre-toothed tiger

 A Megaloceros

 A mammoth

* During this Ice Age, Earth's temperatures were around 5°C lower than average temperatures today.
* Sea levels were low as water turned to ice.
* There have been several Ice Ages — the last one ended around 12,000 years ago.

# The Stone Age, 1 million years ago

It's the Stone Age and early people are living a simple life sheltering in caves and hunting animals for food. George is impressed by his ancestors' cave art whilst Milly takes a nap wrapped up in animal furs. The cavemen are sharpening their flint-stone tools and have learnt how to make fire. Have a look for:

A bison
cave drawing

A pile of
animal bones

A shy mouse

Wood for
the fire

* The Stone Age was so called because early man used stones to make sharp tools.
* The oldest known tools that have been found are 3.3 million years old.
* It is believed that humans first lived in the area that is now Ethiopia, in Africa.

# The Bronze Age, The City of Ur, 2040 BC

The City of Ur in Mesopotamia is ruled by king Ur-Nammu and people here are learning to write for the first time in history. They have also discovered how to turn copper and tin into bronze by melting the metals together over fire. They trade their bronze goods with neighbouring peoples. George points out these interesting things to Milly:

Writing on wet clay

Men trading bronze tools

Mud bricks

The Ziggurat of Ur temple

* The Bronze Age cuneiform script was one of the first forms of writing.
* Mesopotamia was an area in what is now the Middle East.
* People of the City of Ur worshipped the god of the moon, 'Sin' or 'Nanna'.

# Ancient Egypt, 1330 BC

The year is 1330 BC and Pharaoh Tutankhamun rules over Ancient Egypt. Life revolves around the Nile river and the common people here work hard, building and farming. The nobles live a life of luxury and Ankhesenamun the queen wears lots of beautiful gold jewellery. The Ancient Egyptians built magnificent temples in honour of their many gods. Look out for:

The Sphinx

A temple

The Nile river

The Great Pyramid at Giza

* The Great Pyramid at Giza was completed in around 2560 BC, as a tomb for the Pharaoh Khufu. Near it lies the Sphinx statue, with a human head and a lion's body.
* The Egyptian alphabet contained more than 700 hieroglyph (picture) symbols.

# Ancient Greece, 700 BC

The ancient Olympic Games are taking place here in Olympia, Greece, and George and Milly are enjoying the show. Milly recognizes many of the events, as the running races, discus throw, wrestling, boxing and horse riding still take place in the Olympics today. The winner of each event is crowned with an olive wreath. The spectators have their eyes on:

 A sprint champion

 A discus thrower with a bad aim

 A dancing horse

 A wrestling match

* Kyniska of Sparta was the first woman Olympic victor. She trained a winning chariot team.
* The Ancient Olympic games were held in honour of Zeus, the Greek king of the gods.
* Hoplitodromos was a running race for competitors wearing armour!

# The Hanging Gardens of Babylon, 600 BC

George and Milly are in ancient Babylon, exploring its famous Hanging Gardens. These lush royal gardens were planted in terraces set at different levels. The gardens were built by King Nebuchadnezzar II for his wife, Queen Amytis. Milly enjoys stretching her legs as she runs past:

A gardener   A water pump

Two
pink flowers   A doorway made
out of a tree root

* The Hanging Gardens of Babylon are one of the Seven Wonders of the Ancient World.
* The city of Babylon was located in what is now Iraq, but no one has been able to establish the exact site of the Gardens.

# Imperial China, 221 BC

Emperor Qin, the first Emperor of China, built an army of terracotta warriors to protect him in the afterlife after his death. George and Milly are at risk of getting lost amidst the lines of 8,000 warriors and 650 horses, so help them navigate through the corridors of statues. Look out for:

The tallest statue

A smiling horse statue

A musician statue

A chariot with a broken wheel

* The clay soldiers were discovered in 1974 by workers outside the city of Xi'an.
* It is believed that the statues were covered in brightly coloured paint when first made.
* Emperor Qin united a collection of kingdoms to form the first Chinese dynasty.

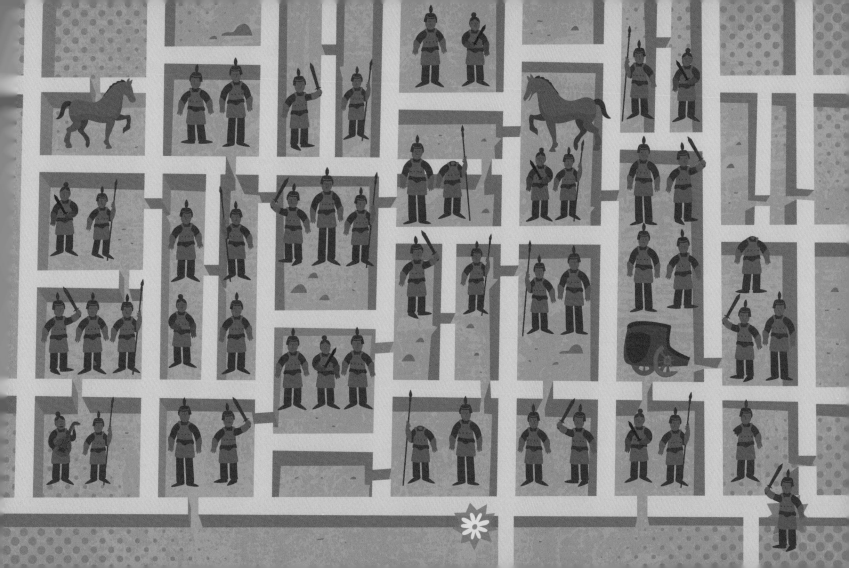

# The Roman Republic, 45 BC

Julius Caesar was a politician and military general who became head of the Roman Republic. He ruled with the support of his friend Mark Antony and fell in love with the Egyptian queen, Cleopatra. He extended the Roman Republic from Rome, in what is now Italy, across much of Europe and the top of northern Africa. But his power was disliked by many and he was assassinated (killed) in 44 BC. See if you can spot:

Mark Antony

Julius Caesar

Servants serving grapes

Queen Cleopatra

* Caesar introduced the Julian calendar, which is very similar to the Gregorian calendar that most of the world now uses.
* Caesar's face was depicted on Roman coins.

# The Roman Empire, AD 60

After Julius Caesar died, Rome was ruled by emperors. Roman armies conquered many countries such as Britain, and then enforced the Roman way of life by building roads and houses, public baths and water supplies. George and Milly are in the middle of a battle on British soil. Boudicca, queen of the Iceni tribe, is leading a revolt against the Roman army. Look out for:

Roman archers

Boudicca, queen of the Iceni tribe

A Roman centurion

Romans behind their shields

* Roman soldiers fought in lines, marching towards the enemy with their shields held in front.
* Roman soldiers used a short sword for stabbing and a long spear for throwing.
* Boudicca's revolt was eventually quashed by the Romans in AD 60 or 61.

# Constantinople, Byzantine Empire, AD 550

George and Milly are in the city of Constantinople (what is now Istanbul in Turkey). It's AD 550, and during the reign of Emperor Justinian I, Constantinople leads the world in art, science, trade and architecture. The city's religion is Christian, its organization is Roman and its culture is Greek. Can you spot:

A bustling harbour

The Hagia Sophia Cathedral

The Roman bath house

The Hippodrome (for chariot racing)

* In AD 324 Emperor Constantine moved the capital of the Roman Empire from Rome to Constantinople.
* The city was the centre of Christianity and Hagia Sophia was the largest cathedral in the world for 1,000 years.
* Justinian I is famous for rewriting and improving the Roman code of law.

# The Mayan Civilization, AD 700

George and Milly have been transported to Central America to Tikal, the centre of the Mayan civilization. The Mayan people write using hieroglyphics and are skilled at art. They are famous for their textiles, pottery, sculptures, murals and baskets. George takes some time to admire the art on display:

A Mayan calendar

A decorated stele (stone)

A carved pot

A sculpture of the maize god

* Many artworks were created to honour gods, such as Itzamna the god of fire and creator of the Earth.
* Mayans also enjoyed music and dancing and used wind instruments, drums and rattles.
* Maize was one of the Mayan people's main crops.

# The Anglo-Saxons, AD 878

After the Romans left Britain in AD 410, the Anglo-Saxons travelled from north-western Europe to settle there. They divided the land into kingdoms and Alfred the Great was king of the southern part of England. George and Milly get a taste of Anglo-Saxon life as they pass:

Houses with thatched roofs

A weaver's loom

A farmer with an ox and plough

Ornate brooches to fasten women's tunics

* The Anglo-Saxons were made up of three different tribes: the Angles, Saxons and Jutes.
* Alfred is the only English king or queen to be known as 'The Great'.
* The Danes wanted to conquer England as well but Alfred fought and defeated them in the Battle of Edington in AD 878.

# The Vikings, AD 930

George and Milly have arrived in Norway just as a group of Viking warriors are setting sail. They want to sneak onto the longboat as it might help them in their quest to get home. They need to avoid being spotted by Eric Bloodaxe, though, as this fearsome Viking warrior is taking his men on an expedition to conquer foreign lands. Can you navigate George and Milly towards the boat? If you're on the right path you'll pass:

Viking coins

A Viking brooch

A drinking horn

A yellow and red striped shield

* The Vikings were seafarers who travelled from their homelands in Scandinavia around much of northern Europe to trade goods and conquer lands.
* The Viking Age lasted from around AD 700 to 1100.
* Eric Bloodaxe was King of Norway and later King of Northumbria in Britain.

# The Battle of Hastings, England, 1066

It's 1066 in England and George and Milly have arrived at a time of great change. Edward the Confessor has just died, passing the English crown to Harold Godwinson. But William of Normandy, France, wants the crown for himself and has sailed to England. A battle commences near Hastings. Harold is killed and William the Conqueror becomes king of England. Look out for:

William on his horse

A soldier hiding under his shield

Harold with an arrow in his eye

An archer shooting three arrows

* Halley's Comet passed over England in 1066 and was thought to be a sign of change.
* The Normans were originally Viking raiders who settled in the north of France.
* An embroidered piece of cloth, 70 m long and known as The Bayeux Tapestry, shows the events of 1066 in pictures.

# A Medieval Castle, France, 1200

Across Europe in Medieval times, kings were often away fighting and they needed lords to keep their land safe in their absence. The lords built castles as homes and fortresses. To stop attackers getting in, many castles had a moat, a drawbridge and tall towers with small windows. Inside, castles were busy places. George and Milly are on a tour of this castle. Look out for:

The great hall

The dungeons

The lord's chamber

An archer at the top of a tower

* Castles were often built on high ground to give a good view of the surrounding land.
* The castle toilet was called the *garderobe* and was a chute leading into the moat.
* Around 150 people lived and worked inside a typical castle.

# Genghis Khan and the Mongol Empire, 1225

Genghis Khan was founder of the Mongol Empire. He united the tribes of northeast Asia, and then travelled the vast expanse of Central Asia and China seizing further territory. He was a ruthless leader, known for killing anyone who got in his way, so George and Milly had better sneak past him without being spotted! Try this route:

Sneak behind the back of Genghis Khan

Pass the horseman with a blue shirt

Turn left at the silk trader

Run past the yurts

* The Mongol Empire covered around 24,000,000 sq km of land at its peak.
* The Mongols fought battles on horseback.
* The Silk Road was formally established under Genghis Khan, allowing the trade of silks between China and Europe.

# Easter Island, Rapa Nui, 1300

This is the tiny island of Rapa Nui in the Pacific Ocean. Polynesian people travelled a huge distance from their South Pacific islands on small, wooden canoes to discover this tiny island a few hundred years ago. They are building mysterious *moai* statues out of huge blocks. Look out for:

 The statue with only a head

 The blindfolded statue

 The statue with a pointy nose

 The Polynesian holding two ropes

* The island is over 3,500 km west of the South American mainland and 2,075 km from the nearest inhabited island.
* It is thought Easter Island was first settled around AD 800 or possibly later.
* The *moai* statues may have been built in honour of the people's ancestors or chiefs.

# Gutenberg's Printing Press, 1441

Johannes Gutenberg invented one of the most important machines ever - the printing press. Before this, books had been printed by hand - a very slow process. The printing press pressed paper onto movable letters covered in ink to create pages of text in no time at all. It's a busy day at the printing press, and George and Milly have been asked to:

Ink the press

Stack the paper

Sort the metal letters

Read the finished books

* Gutenberg made the first press in Mainz, Germany, in 1440.
* A typical press could print 3,600 pages a day.
* Within a few decades the printing press had spread to over 200 cities across Europe.

# The Aztecs, Mexico, 1460

George and Milly are transported to Tenochtitlan in Mexico where Moctezuma I is the ruler. The city is built on a swampy island because it was said that the Aztecs should settle where they saw an eagle holding a snake while perched on a cactus. Poor people farm the land and live in huts. The rich live in brick houses painted white. Can you spot:

Templo Mayor

The market place

The Sun Stone

The palace

* Feathers were a sign of wealth for the Aztecs and used in art and clothing.
* The largest temple in the city was Templo Mayor.
* One god worshipped by the Aztecs was Quetzalcoatl, a feathered serpent.

# The Incas, Peru, 1490

The Inca Empire's capital was Cusco, in Peru, and at the centre of the city was the Coricancha temple complex. This Temple of the Sun was built to worship Inti, the Sun God. The Incans believed he was the supreme god and everything in his temple is covered in gold. George has to put his sunglasses on! Look out for:

The sun mask

The jewelled image of Inti

The praying Incan man

The temple's golden garden

* The Incan Empire covered a large area of western South America from 1438–1533.
* The Incan emperor, known as Inca Sapa, was said to be a descendent of Inti.
* The Incas thought solar eclipses occurred when Inti was unhappy with them.

# Columbus and the Age of Discovery, 1492

Christopher Columbus was a famous explorer who voyaged across the Atlantic Ocean to the Americas to discover new land and claim it for Spain. Columbus opened up a whole new world for Europeans, but this didn't end well for the local people who were taken captive, caught European diseases or were killed in resulting wars. Look out for Columbus's important navigation tools:

A compass

A traverse board

A quadrant

A half-hour glass

* Columbus sailed in the *Santa Maria*, with two other ships, the *Nina* and the *Pinta*.
* The ship carried salted fish, cheese and live pigs and chickens as food for the long journey.
* Columbus's first journey across the Atlantic to the Bahamas took over a month.

# The Ottoman Empire, Istanbul, 1502

George and Milly are back in Constantinople. Almost 1,000 years have passed and the Romans are no longer in control – it's now part of the Ottoman Empire. The Ottoman leader, Mehmet II, has renamed the city Istanbul and built the Grand Bazaar. The bazaar is an important trading site – where goods from far and wide are sold. Many things are being traded here today, including:

 Silk from China

 Grape vines from Europe

 Spices from India

Wool from Central Asia

* Osman I was a nomadic Turkman chief who founded the Ottoman Empire around 1300.
* The Ottomans were Muslims and the name Istanbul means 'city of Islam'.
* The Ottoman Empire was also known as the Turkish Empire.

# The Italian Renaissance, 1504

George and Milly have now reached Italy in the 1500s, a period of great achievement in the arts and sciences, known as the Renaissance. Leonardo da Vinci was one of the most skilful painters of this era. George and Milly are watching him paint his most famous picture – the *Mona Lisa*. Can you spot these items in his studio:

Da Vinci's sketch book

A pile of picture frames

The messy paint palette

The blue splat of paint on the floor

* People still haven't decided whether the lady in the *Mona Lisa* painting is smiling or not!
* The lady in the painting doesn't have any eyebrows.
* Leonardo da Vinci was also an architect, engineer, mathematician, scientist and inventor.

# Elizabethan England, 1600

Our friends are exhausted now and need a night off. Good job they've arrived at the theatre in time to watch a comedy. They are in good company – Queen Elizabeth I of England is here too, and the play is written by William Shakespeare – perhaps the greatest playwright of all time. Look out for these characters:

Queen Elizabeth I

The character with a donkey's head

The acting dog

William Shakespeare

* Elizabeth I was Queen of England and Ireland from 1558–1603.
* Shakespeare wrote 37 plays.
* The character of Bottom has his head transformed into a donkey's head in the play *A Midsummer Night's Dream*.

# Isaac Newton and Gravity, 1666

The year is 1666 and Isaac Newton is sitting under an apple tree in his mother's country garden in Lincolnshire, when an apple falls on his head. Newton wonders why the apple has fallen down and not sideways or upwards. He goes on to work out the law of gravity - what goes up must come down! Look out for:

The pink apple

Newton's apple

The maggot in an apple

The apple with three leaves

* Isaac Newton was an English physicist and mathematician who studied at the University of Cambridge, England.
* Newton realized that an unseen force — gravity — attracts all objects towards each other and that it was drawing the apple towards Earth.

# Pirates in the Caribbean Seas, 1717

Look out! George and Milly better head below deck quickly as the ship they have landed on is the scene of a battle. Blackbeard's pirates have attacked a Spanish merchant ship in search of treasure. The battle is fierce with the pirates firing pistols and waving cutlasses at the scared sailors. Blackbeard has instructed his pirates to do the following — are they succeeding?

Climb the crow's nest

Grab the treasure chest

Raise the skull and crossbones flag

Tie up the captain

* Blackbeard was a feared pirate whose real name was Edward Teach.
* It is said he put smoking fuses in his black beard and hair to scare sailors.
* Blackbeard's ship was called the *Queen Anne's Revenge*.

# The Edo Period, Japan, 1765

It's time for tea on George and Milly's time travel adventure – Japanese green tea. They're in Japan during the Edo Period when nobles attended tea ceremonies hosted by ladies called geisha. The geisha wear beautiful clothes and paint their faces white. They sing, dance, play instruments and games with the guests, and today they are entertaining the Shogun, the leader of Japan. Look out for:

A shamisen instrument

Japanese green tea

The Shogun

A konpira fune fune game

* Geisha wear kimonos made out of beautiful silks that are tied with an *obi* belt.
* The arts flourished during the Edo Period in Japan, with writers, painters and theatres becoming very popular.
* The Shoguns were military leaders who ruled Japan between 1185 and 1868.

# Captain Cook discovers Australia, 1770

It's the year 1770 in Australia. The land has been inhabited by Aboriginal people for 40,000 years, but this is the first time that Europeans have set foot on the continent to colonize it. Captain Cook names his landing site Botany Bay because of the variety of plants he and his men find. Can you spot these things found by Cook:

Kangaroos

Eucalyptus trees

Aboriginal Australians

Banksia flowers

* Captain Cook's ship was called the *Endeavour*.
* Botany Bay is just south of Sydney. Although Botany was intended as the main settlement, Sydney was later chosen as a better location.
* Captain Cook claimed Australia for Britain, not understanding that the local people had already claimed the land as their own.

# The Declaration of Independence, USA, 1776

It's 1776 and America has overthrown British rule and is establishing an independent nation. George and Milly have arrived to see members of the 13 American Colonies gathered together to sign the Declaration of Independence that frees them to form the United States of America. In the room are these famous American statesmen:

George Washington

John Adams

Thomas Jefferson

Benjamin Franklin (who was also a scientist)

* Independence Day is celebrated on the 4th of July, the date when the Declaration was adopted.
* One of the statements in the document famously says that 'all men are created equal'.
* George Washington became the first American President; John Adams was the second, and Thomas Jefferson the third.

# The French Revolution, 1789

Meanwhile, in France, ordinary people have started a revolution to get rid of the ruling upper class. They are angry about paying too much tax and having no say in how the country is run. George and Milly are in Paris in 1789 as rioters attack the Prison of Bastille. The rebellion will spread across France and in 1793 King Louis XVI will be sent to his death. Look for these rioters:

An angry farmer

The man leading the chants

A child beating a drum

The lady waving the French flag

* The French Revolution lasted from 1789—1799.
* 97% of the population were poor peasants who were fed up with being ruled by the elite.
* King Louis XVI and his wife Marie Antoinette had their heads chopped off by a guillotine.

# The Industrial Revolution, Britain, 1820

At the end of the 1700s, life changed in Britain. New machines were invented that could make goods, such as cloth, using steam power, fueled by coal. In this 'Industrial Revolution', people started to work in factories rather than on the land. The invention of the steam engine and railways transported goods around the country quicker than ever before. Can you spot:

A canal boat filled with cloth

The only chimney not spouting smoke

A cloud of smoke shaped like a ship

The carriage holding lots of coal

* The invention of the power loom and other machines greatly speeded up production.
* James Watt created steam engines that powered trains, machines and ships.
* The Industrial Revolution quickly spread to other European countries and the USA.

# The Treaty of Waitangi, New Zealand, 1840

*Nau mai!* Welcome to New Zealand, George and Milly! It's the year 1840 and the leaders of the 125,000 Maoris who live in New Zealand have just signed a treaty with the British king to become a formal British colony. George and Milly watch as the Maoris celebrate. George enjoys watching these traditional Maori events:

 A *hongi* greeting

 A *waka* canoe

 A *kapa haka* dance

 Cooking in the *hangi* underground oven

The Waitangi Treaty had three main points:
* The King or Queen of Britain has the right to rule over New Zealand.
* Maori Chiefs are allowed to keep their land.
* Maori and British subjects both have the same rights.

# American Pioneers, USA, 1850

After the American War of Independence, some people from the east coast of the country moved west to settle new land. These brave pioneers packed all their belongings into wagons and headed into the unknown. Our friends are joining them today. Life was often tough and dangerous, but rewards came as some pioneers made a better life for themselves. Spot the pioneers who are:

Building a new house

Cowboys riding ahead

Part of a wagon trail

Talking with Native Americans

* Pioneers could travel all the way from the east to the west coast along the Oregon Trail.
* They travelled through country already settled by Native Americans.
* They faced cold winters, wild animals, bandits and sometimes hostile Native Americans.

# The American Civil War, USA, 1863

George and Milly are still in America but the country is now at war - with itself. The southern states want to break away from the northern states to form 'The Confederate States of America'. Abraham Lincoln is President and wants the states to stay together and to ban the owning of slaves in the southern states. The battle today is at Gettysburg. Look for:

General Robert E. Lee

The Union flag (northern states)

The secret cannon

The Confederate flag (southern states)

* There were around 51,000 casualties at the Battle of Gettysburg.
* General Robert E. Lee led the Confederate troops.
* The Confederates were defeated at Gettysburg. The Union side won the war in 1865.

# World War One, Europe, 1915

World War One began in Europe in 1914. The warring nations included Britain, France and Russia, who fought against Germany and Austria-Hungary. Soldiers on the front lines lived in trenches in the ground. They sneaked across No Man's Land at night to attack the enemy at first light. George and Milly walk the front line and are shocked at the bad conditions the soldiers have to live in:

Rats are everywhere

Soldiers sleep underground

The trench is wet and muddy

Building the trenches is dangerous work

* Most trenches were around 4 m deep and 1-2 m wide. They were reinforced with sandbags and barbed wire.
* The distance between enemy trenches could be as little as 30 m.
* World War One lasted from 1914—1918.

# The Russian Revolution, 1917-1918

Russia struggled during World War One and in early 1917 a riot broke out due to food shortages. The unrest escalated, leading to the abdication of Tsar (king) Nicholas II. The Bolsheviks took power after promising 'peace, land and bread'. A new 'communist' government was formed, headed by the Bolshevik leader Lenin. Here he is speaking to crowds in Moscow, the capital. Look for:

St Basil's Cathedral

Vladimir Lenin

Bolshevik soldiers

The Communist flag

* The Bolsheviks executed Tsar Nicholas II in 1918.
* Communism is a system where the major resources of a country, such as factories, are owned by the state and wealth is divided equally among its citizens.
* The Communists re-formed Russia into a country called the Soviet Union in 1922.

# The Roaring Twenties, USA, 1925

It's the 1920s in America, and the economy is booming. People enjoy themselves by listening to jazz music, dancing the night away or going to the cinema, a new form of entertainment. The invention of gadgets, such as the fridge and vacuum cleaner, has made housework easier so people can spend more time outside the home. George and Milly are in Chicago and enjoying:

Dancing with the flapper girls

Shopping in the large stores

Watching a baseball game

Driving around town in a car

* Flapper girls were young fashionable women who enjoyed socializing and dancing.
* It was illegal to sell alcohol in America in the 1920s but people did it anyway in secret underground bars called 'speakeasies'.
* A popular purchase in the 1920s was the radio.

# World War Two, Europe, 1944

Take cover, George and Milly! The duo are on the coast of France during D-Day – a major event in World War Two when the Allies landed troops on the beaches to begin the liberation of Europe from German control under the Nazis. The troops are approaching under heavy German gunfire and have to get past mines and obstacles laid down by the Germans. Look for:

'Hedgehog' obstacles

Landing craft

German defences

An overturned tank

* D-Day was the biggest seaborne invasion in history, with over 6,000 ships and 160,000 troops.
* The Allies included US, British and Canadian troops and other nationalities.
* D-Day took place on 6 June 1944. World War Two lasted from 1939 to 1945.

# The Cold War, 1957

George and Milly have reached the year 1957 and have the feeling they're being followed. What's going on? Milly spots a camera hidden in a friendly dog's collar and then George realizes – they are in the Cold War era. This was a conflict between the capitalist USA and the 'west', and the communist Soviet Union and the 'east'. The two sides never fought, but they were constantly spying on each other! Spot some spies' gadgets:

Coded letters

Hidden surveillance

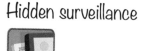

Bugging methods

Concealed messages

* During the Cold War, the Russian spy agency was called the KGB. The US agency, CIA, and the British agency, MI6, still exist today.
* Both sides were worried about the number of nuclear weapons the other side had and if they would ever dare to use them.

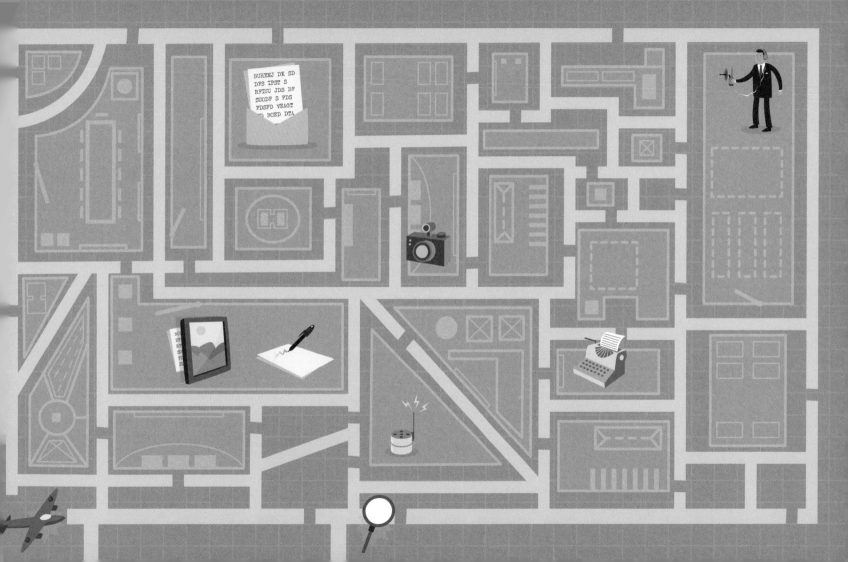

# The First Moon Landing, 1969

"That's one small step for man, one giant leap for mankind."
US astronaut Neil Armstrong has just become the first
person to walk on the Moon as George and Milly watch from
*Apollo 11* command module. For several years the USA and Soviet Union
have been competing to see who can get to the Moon first, to show that
they have the best science and technology. Keep an eye out for:

 'Buzz' Aldrin

 The US flag

 Neil Armstrong

 The *Eagle* landing craft

* Two other men travelled with Armstrong to the
  Moon —'Buzz' Aldrin and Michael Collins.
* Armstrong and Aldrin landed on the Moon in a
  small craft called *Eagle*.
* The landing took place at the Sea of Tranquility.

# Nelson Mandela, South Africa, 1990

Today, a man named Nelson Mandela has been released from prison in South Africa. George and Milly soon learn that this is a momentous occasion as he was imprisoned for resisting apartheid – a system of racial segregation. Non-white people have had restricted rights in South Africa and Nelson has fought to change this so that all people can be equal. Everyone is celebrating, including:

Springboks

Nelson and his wife, Winnie

President de Klerk

Women in traditional dress

* Nelson Mandela was imprisoned for 27 years.
* The end of apartheid meant all citizens had equal rights no matter what colour their skin was.
* South African President de Klerk and Nelson Mandela jointly won the Nobel Peace Prize in 1993 for their work to abolish apartheid.

# Robotic Home, 2030

George wonders if they've finally made it back home – this house looks very like the one in his neighbourhood! But Milly spots something that suggests they have now actually travelled to the future – an electronic gecko robot cleaning the walls! Our friends are in a house of the future where everything is controlled by robots. Look out for this smart technology in the kitchen:

An intelligent fridge

A machine that can print food

An interactive glass note pad

A robot chef

* 'Stickybot' is a climbing robot that looks like a gecko lizard and can help with cleaning.
* Intelligent fridges know what's inside them, can offer recipe ideas and can order more food online.
* 3D printers have been developed that can print food in any shape you want.

# Transport of the Future, 2080

George and Milly are definitely in the future now – this city looks unfamiliar! People in this skyscraper city have flying cars and travel along skyway paths to get around. Even if you still choose to travel at ground level, you don't actually need to drive a car, it does it itself! Milly wants to explore, and what better way to be whisked around town than by the super-speedy maglev train. Look out for:

 A skyscraper in the clouds

 A flying car

 An airship controlling the traffic

 Self-drive cars on the ground

* High-tech companies are developing flying cars that use fans to lift them into the air.
* NASA space agency is planning a 'highway in the sky' in which computers know the route to follow.
* Maglev trains travel at high speeds by magnetically levitating above the tracks to reduce friction.

# Life on Mars, 3015

The date is now 3015 and humans are living on Mars. To breathe freely people must stay inside the safety-domes, but George and Milly are able to walk outside wearing their high-tech space suits. Life outside the human bubble is very different – for one thing, they have to avoid the grumpy little green men! One rocket a month leaves on a journey back to Earth. George and Milly need to board it after passing:

 A Mars Rover

 An alien dog

 A friendly alien

 The raising of the Mars flag

* Mars is the fourth planet from the Sun and has a reddish appearance.
* The average temperature on Mars is about -60°C. Chilly!
* Mars is home to the largest volcano in the Solar System — Olympus Mons is 25 km high.

# Space Tourism, 4016

George and Milly are on the rocket travelling from Mars to Earth when it makes a stop at the Intergalactic Space Station to refuel. The space station is like one huge hotel and guests can use it as a base from which to explore the Solar System. George is tempted to stay, but he's done enough travelling on this trip to last 150 million years! Here's what he could do if he stayed:

Stargaze at galaxies

Join the group travelling to Jupiter

Play a round of golf on the Moon

Research a black hole

* Virgin Galactic is a company developing spacecraft to carry space tourists.
* In the future people may work in space, mining metals from asteroids.
* One day we may see a long distance 'lunar railroad' on the Moon.

# Home, Sweet Home!

When the space rocket lands on Earth, George and Milly are amazed to find they are back in the present year. The space travel must have reset the clock. It seems like a dream but when George checks the date on his phone he finds the photos he took from the eras through history. He and Milly flick through them and remember some of the historical highlights. Can you remember what era these photos are from?

A paintbrush

A skull and cross bones flag

Sprinters

A gecko robot

* George and Milly travelled from 150 million years ago to 2,000 years into the future.
* They met countless famous people!
* They visited the four corners of the Earth, plus the Moon and Mars!

# The Answers

Shhhh!...
TOP SECRET!

**1** A trip to the Natural History Museum

**3**
## An Ice Age,
## 2.5 million years ago

**2**
## The Dinosaurs,
## 150 million years ago

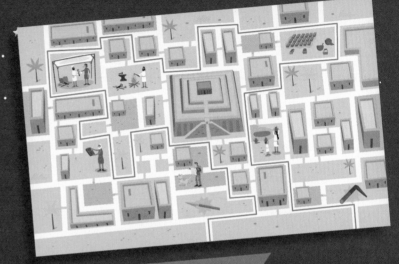

The Bronze Age,
The City of Ur, 2040 BC
5

The Stone Age,
1 million years ago
4

6 Ancient Egypt,
1330 BC

7 Ancient Greece,
700 BC

8 The Hanging Gardens
of Babylon, 600 BC

9 Imperial China,
221 BC

The Roman Republic,
45 BC

The Roman Empire,
AD 60

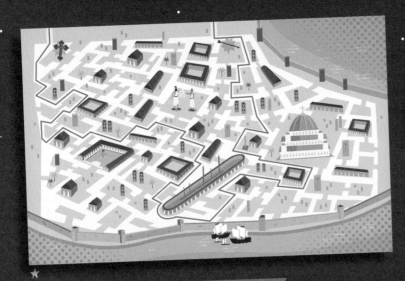

 Constantinople,
Byzantine Empire, AD 550

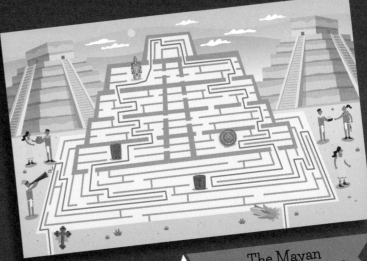

13 The Mayan
Civilization, AD 700

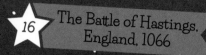
16 The Battle of Hastings, England, 1066

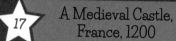
17 A Medieval Castle, France, 1200

18 Genghis Khan and the Mongol Empire, 1225

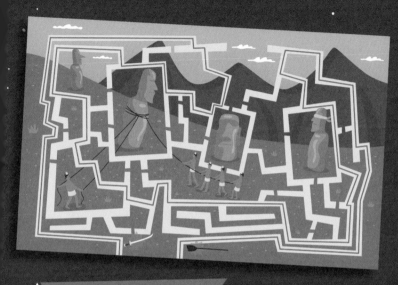

19 Easter Island,
Rapa Nui, 1300

20 Gutenberg's
Printing Press, 1441

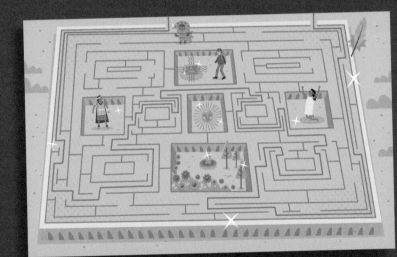

22 The Incas,
Peru, 1490

21 The Aztecs,
Mexico, 1460

23 · Columbus and the Age of Discovery, 1492

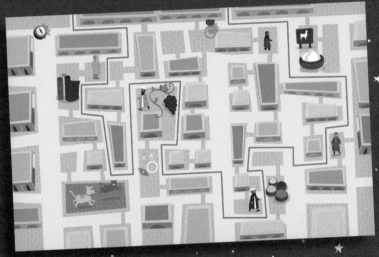

24 · The Ottoman Empire, Istanbul, 1502

25 The Italian Renaissance, 1504

26 Elizabethan England, 1600

27 Isaac Newton
and Gravity, 1666

28 Pirates in the
Caribbean Seas, 1717

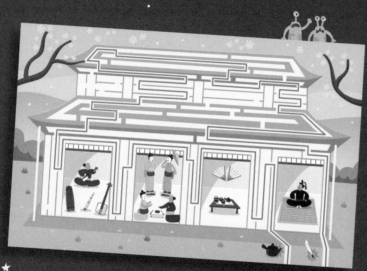

 29 The Edo Period,
Japan, 1765

30 Captain Cook discovers
Australia, 1770

31 The Declaration of Independence, USA, 1776

32 The French Revolution, 1789

33 The Industrial Revolution, Britain, 1820

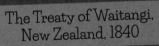 **34** The Treaty of Waitangi,
New Zealand, 1840

**35** American Pioneers,
USA, 1850

World War One,
Europe, 1915

37

The American
Civil War, USA, 1863

36

38 The Russian
Revolution, 1917-1918

39 The Roaring Twenties,
USA, 1925

40 World War Two,
Europe, 1944

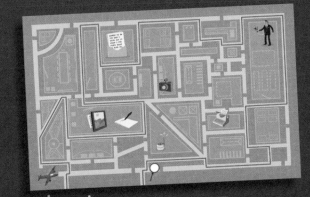

41 The Cold War, 1957

42 The First
Moon Landing, 1969

43 Nelson Mandela,
South Africa, 1990

44 Robotic Home, 2030

Space Tourism, 4016

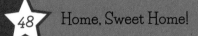

48 Home, Sweet Home!